You
Can Be
the Last
Leaf

You

Can Be

the Last

Leaf

Selected Poems

MAYA ABU AL-HAYYAT

Translated by
Fady Joudah

MILKWEED EDITIONS

Published 2022 by Milkweed Editions
Printed in 2022
Cover design by Mary Austin Speaker
Cover art: *"Olive." Photo etching by Leena Nammari*
22 23 24 25 26   5 4 3 2 1
First Edition

Library of Congress Cataloging-in-Publication Data

Names: Abū al-Ḥayyāt, Māyā, author. | Joudah, Fady, 1971-
    translator.
Title: You can be the last leaf : selected poems / by Maya Abu Al-
    Hayyat ; translated Fady Joudah.
Description: First edition. | Minneapolis, Minnesota : Milkweed
    Editions, 2022. | Summary: "Translated from the Arabic and
    introduced by Fady Joudah, You Can Be the Last Leaf draws
    on two decades of work to present the transcendent and timely
    US debut of Palestinian poet Maya Abu Al-Hayyat"-- Provided
    by publisher.
Identifiers: LCCN 2021037289 (print) | LCCN 2021037290
    (ebook) | ISBN 9781571315403 (trade paperback ; acid-free
    paper) | ISBN 9781571317513 (ebook)
Subjects: LCSH: Abū al-Ḥayyāt, Māyā--Translations into English. |
    LCGFT: Poetry.
Classification: LCC PJ7908.A44 Y68 2022 (print) | LCC PJ7908.
    A44 (ebook) | DDC 892.7/1--dc23
LC record available at https://lccn.loc.gov/2021037289
LC ebook record available at https://lccn.loc.gov/2021037290

Milkweed Editions is committed to ecological stewardship. We strive to
align our book production practices with this principle, and to reduce
the impact of our operations in the environment. We are a member of the
Green Press Initiative, a nonprofit coalition of publishers, manufacturers,
and authors working to protect the world's endangered forests and
conserve natural resources. *You Can Be the Last Leaf* was printed on acid-
free 30% postconsumer-waste paper by Versa Press.

Contents

III. (from *That Smile, That Heart*, 2012)

IV. (from *What She Spoke of Him*, 2006)

You

Can Be

the Last

Leaf

Foreword

Maya Abu Al-Hayyat was born in Beirut to a Palestinian father and a Lebanese mother. She lives in Arabic and resides in Jerusalem. In her poetry we search for what we already know but can't or won't find. If we find it, all the better:

> we the pursued
> over our identities,
> our places of birth,
> and especially our burial lots,
> we, kind and wicked.

You Can Be the Last Leaf opens with "My House," an encounter with biography between the magical, which ruptures temporality, and the archival that catalogs it. A poet's house is language, and Abu Al-Hayyat is relentlessly direct in everything she speaks: when she patiently assembles her soul or when she leaps through it. Even in her first poetry collection, *What She Spoke of Him* (2006)—a hello-goodbye to the lyric of myth between her lips—we sense her movement toward the "looming wide path" that's become her own style of clarity. She was a young Palestinian woman in love then, whose beloved was shot dead by Israeli forces on the first day of the second intifada in Nablus in 2000: "the hegemonic place / slapped [her] heart." This biographical detail is not explicit in the book. The relationship between tragedy and love is not the poet's alone and remains an ongoing reality for countless Palestinians. Yet the journey she takes from the first collection to the fourth, from "The Upcoming Dervish Dance" to "Some Microbes" or "Revision," for example, is astonishing.

1

In *The Last Leaf* the exteriors of the self are mounted on a carousel along with other selves. The allure of these poems is simple. They illuminate the inseparability of private and public domains within a forcibly imposed and constricted, indeed strangled, space. Sometimes shrewd humor on the edge of frivolity offers the poet breathing room.

> My demands are basic,
> some patting on my head
> and clemency for my horrible daily deeds.
> Like a domestic animal
> I wait for their surplus kindness,
> their quick petting that heralds
> my self-removal from their vicinity
> before they get bored
> and toss me aside.

The multifarious Palestinian voice lives on in Maya Abu Al-Hayyat's words, ordinary as grief and daily as laughter. Recurrence and reverberation—at the level of structure, motif, vocabulary, or imagination—toy with negligence and forgetting. She juggles irony "with the skill of a plagiarist / who knows what to add and what to delete / for the text to become original." She asks "how you crossed the street / after you were released / from long detention" and answers: "like a miracle." She burns time like tires at checkpoints where she writes her novel about a butcher who wants to be a violinist. And in the taxi that takes her from or to the checkpoint, she meditates on roads of loss that always lead to a settlement—or to love: "your panting heart, / I heard it today in a radio song."

Though she is a novelist, she is hesitant to pick up the thread of story in her poems. It is less a question of dipping in the same well twice than of shielding herself from unraveling in the breath of verse: "Massacres teach me not to wait / for those who'll be pulled out of the rubble." Still she insists on registering small things in her "supermarket of a purse" where she repossesses the stolen items from her sphere of rights. What she sees does not turn her into a seer. She mocks heroism, dislikes "great" men, and believes in smiling ear to ear whenever she can believe in nothing. You will hear and taste her laughter and also yours. Because laughter is "the excess knowledge no one takes seriously," the cherished identity smuggled out of psychology and surveilled consciousness. The poet celebrates survival as a last leaf in autumn is sister to the first leaf in spring.

Maya Abu Al-Hayyat lives in "a phobia called hope" and all "the disappointments / that were committed in its name." She is daring in self-criticism without internalizing self-mutilation: "I've never blamed my nails / for nails that tear the flesh on my back." Her compassion is "aware some people suffer enough torment to become a lighthouse / then live on to old age / incapable of seeing what lights their way." In most of these poems clarity releases cogitation like pigeons. "Madness advocates for truth." Why not then an elegy for the desire of mothers? Even if all this life on earth "the universe digests / unaffected," it's still the same universe that "whimpers" when a child's smile is erased from this world: "Those who win by killing fewer children / are losers."

The cunning brutality of Israeli colonialism trickles down to aspirations for the colonized to be in "good standing in a middle class / that guards itself against a painful death." The poet has the measure of civilization's pulse, its insatiable desire for supremacy, and its "electronic products / that will enhance your solitude / without increasing your loneliness." So she pleads with art instead: "Only you can lie / as you tell the truth / and make it possible." Her capacity to unfold history and politics is uncanny:

Oh My We've Grown

and can tell
a Kurdish tune from an Iraqi one.

Whoever invented
squeezing breasts with a bra,
that maker of this great prison,
should be prosecuted.

A poet from Palestine, she moisturizes time, bombards it with laundry, cleans up vomit, and can't walk away from humor even when contemplating death—by some "virus heretofore unknown. / Or a well-known virus that doctors and pharmacists got bored with / and missed its reappearance." And if all else fails, the end will come in the form of "a famine [in which] our spouses will eat us." Maya Abu Al-Hayyat is a generous spirit, fierce and funny. Her lucidity is arresting. She asserts her liberation. She loses everything to deserve the title of lover and then watches clouds pass.

Fady Joudah

I.

(from *The Book of Fear,* 2021)

My House

None of the many houses I lived in
concern me. After the third house
I lost interest, but lately my organs and body parts
have been complaining of inexplicable ailments.
My arms extend higher than a tree.
My acromegaly. And when I run
it's at inconsistent speeds.
The important thing is to pass those walking
closest to me, leave them behind
before they leave me.
A Tunisian doctor
told my dad "It's a psychiatric condition."
I had liked her and considered her a house
before she spoke that sentence
which caused a lot of bruises
and brought down the house.
I read several texts I took for houses
and stayed in them a while: *Liquid Mirrors*
was a crazy abode in which I forgot
my first love. There were magazines, too:
Al-Karmal, Poets, Aqwass,
then I studied engineering,
specialized in earthquakes
to build houses whose foundations
resist climates and the unpredictable.
My children dug up a trench for me
and said, "Here, rest a bit, Mom."
But trenches leave marks on skin
as on a field, and the birds

gathered, pecked my seeds
after the field had drowned in stagnant water.
In a text, I can build a house
with windows and balconies
that overlook galaxies and stars,
paint it with the writings of Amjad Nasser
who said that for the sake of a solid house
one should distinguish
between imagination and knowledge
even if the house is built on illusion.
I will raise my house on the backs of horses
that will carry it to the fields,
there my legs will pause.

A Road for Loss

Like the rest of you
I thought of escape.
But I have a fear of flying,
a phobia of congested bridges
and traffic accidents,
of learning a new language.
My plan's for a simple getaway,
a small departure:
pack my children in a suitcase
and to a new place we go.
Directions confuse me:
there's no forest in this city,
no desert either.
Do you know a road for loss
that doesn't end
in a settlement?
I thought of befriending animals,
the adorable type, as substitutes
for my children's electronic toys,
but I want a place for getting lost.
My children will grow,
their questions will multiply,
and I don't tell lies,
but teachers distort my words.
I don't hold grudges,
but neighbors are always nosy.
I don't rebuke,
but enemies kill.
My children grow older,

and no one's thought yet
to broadcast the final news hour,
shut down religious channels,
seal school roofs and walls,
end torture.
I don't dare to speak.
Whatever I speak of happens.
I don't want to speak.
I'd rather be lost.

What If

Every time I leave the house,
it's suicide.
And each return, a failed attempt.
What if burning tires exploded
and the soldiers went rogue?
What if teenagers turned radical
and the truck driver dozed off
at the wheel? What if
I find what I'm looking for?
I want to return home whole.
I mark the roads with crumbs
to help me come and go
until the birds
eat all my bread.

Ordinary Grief

I loved you, my love,
there's no doubting or denying it,
no justification or synopsis,
there isn't even a story behind it.
It was a collision.
The stairway was rising,
the heavens descending,
and the roads had softened.
I loved you, my love,
as words gather in a poem
and remain forever,
immortal, true, and quotable.
And just as death ceases to be
a logo of end or separation,
I loved you for life
to become elegant, dignified,
useful, for the seasons
to succeed one another
rhythmic and precise,
for cruelty to rationalize
our capacity to resist, endure.
There's no doubt or denial.
Look at them, my sighs
as they rise for twenty years.
And check my gaze that recognizes
you in an instant
whenever you pass in a breeze,
look at my steps as they break
over sidewalks and king-size beds,

and you'll know, my love,
that I loved you
without evidence,
motive, or demand.

From, To

I run away from sunglassed martyrs
in posters on city walls
to the happy endings in children's stories

and from the burrow of the anxious mother mole
in my head, who gnaws at me
with poems about love or lack of love,

and I aim at her
a stray bullet of a teenage soldier
I encounter daily at the checkpoint

where we practice
the proper glower
to face an enemy with.

Fear

I am therefore
they point their rifles at me.
Out of their eyes and fingertips I come gushing.
They toss me over the laborers' drowsy eyes
and tired shoulders
then carry me in their passports
and biographies. So I wander with them
as they terrify children
and startle mothers from sleep at night.
You're looking
straight into my eyes so that I may
dispatch teenagers to the army
and shape their future.
Here I am armed on street corners,
inside tanks, on the roofs,
staring into space, omnipresent, constantly working,
dispossessing slumber from its lids,
causing panic, caprice, unintended murder.
Can you address me
with reason, without it all falling apart,
your adages, myths, and creeds?
I am the deliverer of illusory happiness
in solid societies: "See how busy the roads are"
says the taxi driver as he points to the radio:
"Business is booming,
industry's growing, and we're 13th
among the nations."
I pat the driver on the back,
he's trembling in the dark,

rummaging for the bliss of one
who's accepted
that this is as good as it gets.
I am their master's servant:
I lead them to obedience, to faith:
that his order is better
than the chaos that would terminate them.

As long as you stare into my eyes, I shall remain.
As long as you are another.
As long as you are eternal.

Like a Domestic Animal

To gain the favor of homeowners
I gaze sadly into their eyes
and rub their shoulders.
My demands are basic,
some patting on my head
and clemency for my horrible daily deeds.
Like a domestic animal
I wait for their surplus kindness,
their quick petting that heralds
my self-removal from their vicinity
before they get bored
and toss me aside.
And when they're asleep
I do what pleases me
with their persnickety arrangements,
reset their alarm clocks
to my barks and hunger
and door scratching.
Tenderly I listen to no one.
And for approval, curses, and attention
I nip, howl, and roll around.

We

Yes, we
who raise our flags on every occasion,
mention Palestine twenty times in a sentence,
afraid to laugh for too long,
guilty over our fleeting small joys,
we the pursued
over our identities,
our places of birth,
and especially our burial lots,
we, kind and wicked,
heroic and obstinate,
the first to die and, if necessary, the last,
we nationalists, sentimentalists, tearful,
always tearful
over children we don't know
who pass by us
with or without sending smiles our way,
their many questions and infuriating habits.
We showed our hand too soon,
our weeping over adolescents
who peacefully stand in front of their houses
making gestures, playing
the game of men,
and our weeping over mothers, all of them,
the happy ones with news of pregnancy,
and those who dispatch letters to TV
and radio stations, oh mothers
who send winter clothes one size too big
to their incarcerated sons,

yes mothers
who regurgitate their sorrows and mottoes
as stories regurgitate us,
year after year,
we cry and cry
until we cry no more
and stop joking around.
We showed our hand too soon,
we know who we are.

I Don't Ask Anymore

how many kids you have,
where you live,
or what your profession is:
I don't care. Maybe I care
how you spend your day
or pass the long nights in anguish,
how you treat your chronic illness,
seasonal allergies, swellings,
your method with longing,
how you avoid toxic videos
and never stop on the street
when everyone else stops.
Tell me how you crossed the street
after you were released
from long detention—
it matters to me
what you're thinking now
as you coerce your kids to sleep
in the middle of shelling,
as you sweep off them
the ghost of death in nightmares.
I don't ask anymore
about your land or religion,
maybe I care
how you were tortured
in the first or second intifada
and other wars. How you took care
of your pills and fears,
escaped destiny by chance,

through teargas,
incursions,
and the tank in the city square.
Your name, your age,
what you look like don't matter.
You passed through here
like a miracle.

Massacres

Massacres teach me not to wait
for those who'll be pulled out of the rubble
and not to follow the stories of survivors.
I go on with my day without pausing for wonders.
I've learned how friends forget me
and, if I'm lucky, my enemies as well.
Callously I pass through memories.
Love on the faces
of adolescent girls also passes,
makeup and sorrow eat it.
And the orphanage within the suitcases of orphans
is tossed by slogans to the rubbish bins of poetry.
Nothing's forever.
Not success or laziness,
not dithering or labor,
even dazzling verse
grows onerous,
and to stumble or shatter
is sometimes beautiful.
A little bit of weight gain,
a fainting glimmer in the eyes,
some friends who evade or desire you,
there's not much more to learn.
I keep running in empty rooms
to begin my day as if yesterday didn't end
and tomorrow won't come.
And before I cast my curses
on those who persevere in loneliness
and hesitate to return my greetings,

I remember how often in the chill
we leave tender skin
bloodied, alien, and dry.

Similarities

Even if what you mean is justice,
pain, or history,
is there a difference?
The hater resembles the hater
and the murderer, the murderer.
An aerially bombed building
looks like the blown-up one.
A child riddled with holes
resembles another torn apart.
A bereaved mother
resembles a mother in waiting.
Is there a difference,
after you drop justice
from your reply? Justice
is the right of all who live
in the wrong places in this world,
the right of the aggrieved,
the weak, and the poor.
It isn't a killer's pretext,
a crutch for the malevolent,
or a sword for the unjust.
Give me a reason
to hand over my kids to you
and resemble the hordes.

Plans

Now and then I lay down plans
to solve the world's problems.

My plans eliminate longing from stories,
remove exhaustion from groans,
place full stops in runaway sentences,
rescue even soldiers at checkpoints
along with children
who grow up in detention centers,
mothers who wear their wardrobes
of patience, and also laborers
who commit suicide
off scaffolds. I save the whole world
as a star might in well-drafted screenplays,
with plans that my impoverished
creativity ultimately kills. My plans,

they would have worked,
they would have saved us all.

Your Laughter

The day you explain your laugh to anyone
should never come. Your laugh would lose
its prestige. Laughter
is the excess knowledge no one takes seriously.
And if someone deplores your peals,
pity them, wish them well,
and go after your chuckles
full throttle.

Return

1.

On Highway 6
between Tel Aviv and Jerusalem,
drivers pay a toll for the well-paved road,
busses on either side
transport passengers who've returned at last
to Ramleh or Lidd, the latter in peace, with jars
for the holy festival of Prophet Saleh.
Justice was walking on the shoulder
of the road outside the yellow line
giving back to the streets their names.

Rahmeh (Mercy) was seven
when she escaped a fire with her quick feet
at the family's annual BBQ
in At-tirah. Now she leans on a cane she rented
from Bashir Hospital
but won't give it back. She's gazing through
the air-conditioned bus: dreams
don't come true through will
or the passage of years that come undone
like rosary beads or a grape cluster
loosened in a bowl for kids.
Years that roll under the bed.
Dreams propel the body forward instead.
Decisions are taken by need—
no matter the arthritis, expenses,
plethora of adolescents, damp walls, and old cots—

because need clips the wings of dreams
and the legs of the righteous.

Rahmeh (Mercy),
who could run barefoot as fast and for as long
as a Kenyan runner might
in the Sydney Olympics,
didn't succumb to dementia or Alzheimer's.
She can still rise to her feet to smell Yafa's sea,
but the smell of grilled meat and hair spray
plug her nose. Death,
the beast we wrap in romance novels
as terrible texts are wrapped
in ornate words, peers
from the other side of the window.
The reflection almost defines
the form of the end.

This may be the last chance.
Highway 6, whose toll you paid,
is your road.

2.

Sunlight penetrates green leaves
like an old brilliance on a dark night.
Badhan Road is winding and treacherous.
Accidents can happen.
A car or rocks may fall
from the top to the bottom.
A flash pierces my sleeping eyes.

This road that leads me to Nablus is astonishing,
this road to my father's return from his exile
to the place I left behind.
A dark-skinned man drives
the seven-seater Mercedes from Jericho.
The vehicle won't stop vibrating.
Badhan Road: What name is this
whose cold waterfalls give
small parks their names,
fill plastic chairs with bottoms that hover
over floating watermelons in a chilly stream?
What world is this
between Jericho and Nablus,
the lowest and highest points?
"This is return," my father says,
with tears in his eye
that a shrapnel from an old war damaged
back when he used to wear khaki.

My father falls
asleep with a pistol,
eats his watermelon slices
without fork or plate
in the Mercedes where other passengers are
scared or asleep. The dark-skinned driver
from Jericho doesn't recognize their fear.
He wants to make it back in time
to add his name to the long list
of drivers for tomorrow's work.

3.

"Are we human?"
the book's yellow cover asks.
We live in what others have designed and dreamt.
We live in what the wind has done to a tree
thousands of years ago,
above animal and scorpion urges,
in the belly of whales, within roots
and echoes, the nightly chatter of cave dwellers.
We roam the streets of engineers and the debris
of sharp axes in drawings
of ancient municipalities
inside the head of a hasty old man.
Our words about the free soul,
beliefs, and the innocent
land are part of the design.
A screw in the mind of the rocking chair
that grants the universe a burst of passion.

4.

They wrote thousands of letters,
hung them to dry
on laundry lines,
and when the wind arrived
it did what it usually does:
erosion, corrosion,
then transfer of the body
and alphabet parts it could carry,
as the heavy parts are left behind disfigured.

This is the reason why
whenever they searched their memory
for a road,
an orange,
an olive,
a view from a window,
they couldn't find it.

That's how myths are made:
erosion, corrosion,
drop by drop,
doggedly, bitterly
they draw memory out.
You don't know how bitter
it is to search
a map for a memory
and find a cadaver.

Some Microbes

Some microbes
liberate themselves
from the body they've settled in
by suicide.
They whisper in your ear
to smash your car into a wall
or blow up a pier.
Even madness,
our singular claim to superiority,
is nothing more than a vitamin deficiency.
All this, and you still doubt
how pink
my nipples are
after I've told you they're pink.
Microbes whisper Vitamin D
to me, whisper amino acids,
yellow plasma, and a man
that morphine takes away
as oxygen grabs him by his arm.
I touch myself to live free
of arterial disease and gastric ailments.
I counter microbes
with supplements
that give me headaches
and good standing in a middle class
that guards itself against a painful death.
I used to fear going hungry

in the cold
of forgetting.
Now I fear microbes with voices.

Ads

The notifications
about illicit drugs
in schools reached me.
All the ads for workshops
that speed up your entry
into someone's heart
are here. And the ads
for diets that will sculpt
your waistline
in a week,
the ads for electronic products
that will enhance your solitude
without increasing your loneliness,
anything that will burn time
reached me. And quickly
I forward them
to my only friend
who's eying
early retirement
to gaze at her heartstrings
in a constellation.

Art

Art is our reparation for love and wisdom,
loss and prospect,
the same art that has destroyed
its makers' minds and fingertips
created everything else in our stead
and left us hungry.
Art that teaches us pain
leaves a mark, but happiness
courses ordinary.
Art that turned orphanhood into a sign
and darkness into a road,
listen to me: I'm aware that all sorts
of machines roll over you,
all kinds of wires above and below ground,
pipes and conduits, arterial
technologies that deprive you of air.
But don't leave us
even if we leave you,
don't turn away your face.
We've behaved like this before,
abandoned life to receive you,
but nothing happened.
You enlivened us,
became our ally in war and exile,
our partner on warm and cold nights
when we were made lonely
or made others lonely.
So don't do it,
whether our voices ebb or flow

on your tenacious modesty,
don't feel ashamed of your beauty
and don't abandon us to monstrosity.
Everything else returns us
to our high cliffs
where life in its maximum elegance
is stretched out between us and death.
Only you can lie
as you tell the truth
and make it possible.

Revision

I must revise my work with the past,
take my time, without malice.
So far I have spread my past, quite well I'd say,
over men and aunties,
and was convinced that I would heal from it
once they were dead
and decomposed,
my ribs a broom
and my hands a canvas.
And especially after I give a lesson
on the imperishable land
and baby chicks that fall out of their nests
just before a crow eats them.
I must revise my work with the past,
my many loves
who died and still possess their corpses,
but also those who died
without declarable bodies.
I will inform them that I distributed the same poem
to each of them, though I didn't necessarily
love them, a point I have previously explained,
that I like to explain again
as I redistribute poems.
I will tell them about your corpse
sprayed with chlorine
in a plastic bag
and how we return.
It wasn't fair that you died
without a last scribble

in which you challenge something,
anything, so that we can say
"He finished his final painting,
didn't leave it suspended in our throats."
Whenever there's a going, there's no return.
They're distributing plastic bags to the masses,
spraying chlorine through massive pumps.
We're carrying our souls
right under our shoulders.

You Can't

They will fall in the end,
those who say you can't.
It'll be age or boredom that overtakes them,
or lack of imagination.
Sooner or later, all leaves fall to the ground.
You can be the last leaf.
You can convince the universe
that you pose no threat
to the tree's life.

II♦

(from *House Dresses and Wars*, 2016)

Lovers Swap Language

the way enemies exchange stabs:
he takes a word from her lexicon
and she takes one from his book.
That's how poems are made
and also bigoted speeches.

And when lovers and enemies sleep,
the ether carries a hot hum
the universe digests
unaffected.

Search

I tidy the room, dust the cushions,
fling open the closet doors
like someone who forgot something between two rudders,
then remember that I once forgot you in my fluffy
nightgown pocket.

I look behind the couches
that extend the length of the wall and windows.
The vase is full of keys, dirt, and telephone bills.
The gas bill will soon double in this cold
and I'm about to go broke.

I listen to the weather forecast one last time.
As I rummage through the kitchen cabinets
I see that I need a new pressure cooker.
Maybe you can leave in it
your intractable diseases.
The sugar in the pantry needs some ants,
and my heart, a vent.

The Kids Are Screaming Now

I listen to their jokes and chatter about God and the Devil,
the flames that burn liars,
and what fluttering beautiful doves are saying.

The kids are screaming now
as I write down all of this with the skill of a plagiarist
who knows what to add and what to delete
for the text to become original.

I draw a sketch of the schoolteacher
who will reprimand me tomorrow
after the kids tell her what I said:
"No God will burn us, and no Devil will live in our hearts."

And through my laptop screen
a hole in my heart the size of the one in the ozone
widens. It fits the kids, the devils, the schoolteacher,
and the one touch from your hand
that can seal it.

Out from under a House Dress

The smell of sex is pungent,
and secret lovers are betrayed
by fragrance.
Simple differences

between scent and perfume,
like the distance between my mouth
and your words,
hushed, planted with knife and thorn.

*

With new recipes I resist
my overwhelming desire
for suicide.
My neighbor, she also does it

by narrating bawdy stories
whose heroine I am.
My friends ignore my messages
of this kind
to keep their days serene.

*

Glaring white,
my dresses hang
on the balcony,
and I offer them to the one and only

garbage collector in the neighborhood,
then run to the bus stop
to buy new everything
except for clothespins.

Mothers Arrange Their Aches at Night

Joint pain, high sugar,
rheumatic ailments,
a boy who missed school because of a cold:
mothers feel sadness for mysterious reasons,
like sadness over other mothers
who stand in public streets
holding photos of their sons'
well-groomed faces
with sideburns and mustaches,
waiting for the cameras to capture them
and their chapped hands.
Mothers who hold up the house beams,
open windows,
air out carpets on roofs,
expel moths from the hearts
of abandoned mattresses
in case a visitor arrives.
Mothers, who stipulate
no conditions for return,
arrange their aches at night
and wash their daughters' hair with oil,
in bed they toss and turn.
And when they fall asleep
they snore
and give the house a name and a voice.

Revolution

The revolutions I've known
began their first day

by drafting lists
for a wall of shame.

Those who win by killing fewer children
are losers.

A land that promises heaven
is an impoverished land.

We Were Young, You Gave Us a Home

that wasn't always warm,
and that was when you gave us
Aladdin's lantern.
We had no money
to fill it with kerosene,
so you got us blankets
to pile on top of blankets.
Hunger stole our sleep,
and you got us lentils and bread
that didn't look like the lentils
and bread on magazine covers,
so you took away the magazines.
Always generous,
even as we fell over like rice grains
on our way to school,
you provided us with a white cloud
so that we may pass in peace,
supplied us with lovestruck eyes
that peered through windows
for ecstasy to grab us.
We had nothing to complain about.
Politely we thanked you as our teacher
had instructed, then she beat us
when we giggled in the bathroom.
We thanked you when we got measles
and when we fell in love.
And when we grew up as if in a race
and asked about the secret of life,
you furnished us with a war

that made us forget
our questions for a few years.
We became mothers
after you'd given us husbands,
became lonely and had children
who doubled our loneliness,
so you gave us more children.
We thanked you when we were sick
and when they were sick
until we got tired of giving thanks
and went back to ask our teacher why
we were so tired.
Then we remembered
that we were young
and that you had given us a home
that wasn't always warm
but had your Aladdin's lantern.

Oh My We've Grown

and can tell
a Kurdish tune from an Iraqi one.

Whoever invented
squeezing breasts with a bra,
that maker of this great prison,
should be prosecuted.

Penniless

Penniless I live at a checkpoint,
trifles make me happy,
like when a whole day passes without me
seeing a single soldier,
his bored yawning.
There I write my new novel
about the butcher
who wanted to be a violinist.
Mean and vulgar,
his hands failed him, favored
the sharp glistening blades.
You can imagine how gloomy it can be
to be destitute, penniless,
to live at a checkpoint,
to know happiness
in trifles, skipping a loquacious poet's turn
in line, or passing wiped out
day laborers with banana sacks
on their backs, guava bags,
and containers of Tnuva milk.
I'm destitute. For years
I've been living in a tomb
but have seen neither angel nor devil,
just more than my share of sleepy soldiers.

I Suffer a Phobia Called Hope

Each time I hear that word
I recall the disappointments
that were committed in its name:
the children who don't return,
the ailments that are never cured,
the memory that's never senile,
all of them hope crushed
beneath its wings as I smash
this mosquito on my daughter's head.

*

The grieving have only the unknown.
It's their only staple and inheritance.
Pain has no logic. All things redeem
the grieving except your rational questions.

*

I wish that no one goes
and no one comes.
All going is a stroke of myth
and each return
a punctured lung.

I Burn Time

like tires at a checkpoint,
alone I choke,
alone I pollute the air.

Nightmares are still budding,
caught in nets,
and I can't stop my urge
to empty my bladder.

Annually you die,
each year in a different manner.
And this year I'm thinking
of your enormous gut:

it was exhausting to tie
your brown shoes.
And your panting heart,
I heard it today in a radio song.

We Could Die in a Traffic Accident

Or after a long protracted illness that makes others wish us dead.
A flash flood might do it after heavy rain.
A forgotten bomb from a previous war
or a fresh bomb from an ongoing one.
A virus heretofore unknown.
Or a well-known virus that doctors and pharmacists got bored with
and missed its reappearance.
We might stop breathing: there are too many of us on the planet.
Or in a famine our spouses will eat us.
And in excess our arteries will clog up.
Smoking kills.
Lack of pleasure.
Too much sex.
A fire from a scented candle.
A depressed driver.
A jealous husband.
A rookie burglar.
And we could die of waiting for death.
Nothing new in any of it,
no insight or learned lessons.
Only the facts
in present and continuing actions.

Sex

Frequently I have wet dreams
with my enemies,
wake up as if I'd just come out of a war,
squeeze my damp thighs in bed
to savor pleasure a little bit more.
And as those dreams recur
I spend my days examining the matter,
following their news,
searching for photos of their wives,
their new cars,
their ceaseless projects,
before I spot them at some crucial moment
crossing the street,
sending me looks or looking away
and hurrying.
Should I hide my face
in my husband's jacket
or behind my children's orange stroller?
This is enmity:
it affords us the luxury
of being forgotten,
though like pleasure
it never forgets us.

My Laugh

I'm exhausted from smuggling my laugh out of my psychology,
smuggling my laugh out of the fates of those I love,
out of videos of slaughtered children
and children who will be kidnapped
from their magical smiles tomorrow,
exhausted from smuggling my laugh
out of sins, ugly secrets,
and in ripped stockings: my jarring laugh
that breaks my ribs
and gashes
public decency.

Since They Told Me My Love
Won't Be Coming Back from the War

I tried everything:
God, for example,
I leaned on his chest and prayed,
and on that rug, once and for all,
I learned that my love
won't come back, and that if he does
won't recognize me.

I tried my hand at politics,
memorized patriotic songs,
befriended legislators,
adored warriors,
but seasonal and moody
they changed their faces
as they do their speeches
once they got close to my pockets.
And then I knew that my love
won't know me even if he returns.

Since they told me my love
won't be coming back from the war,
I've been writing our children's names
on clouds and in journals,
documenting their birthdays,
shoe sizes, the poems they recite,
and once and for all

I learned that all of them
won't be coming back from the war,
and neither will I.

Whistling

Do you see this hole in my neck?
Not sure if it was a bullet or a word that did it.
But I'm certain two lips passed over it
and left a whistling behind.
And also a rustle
whenever I turn
to the future or the past.

Daily I Imagine Them

Those who die in wars that don't concern them,
they were driving through shortcuts
or smoking their cigarettes on the roof,
watching a romantic comedy
or a cooking show,
they were passing through the wrong war
to become numbers and martyrs.

I imagine their sorrow as I cross a checkpoint,
wait for my kids after school,
peel garlic and smell my fingers,
or peek out the window to shoo pigeons away.
And at night in bed
I dream of a war
that's got no war in it.

I'm Not Saying You Lie

You've prepared everything for our death:
shrouds, dreams, and chants,
rockets, hate, and myth.

You rented houses for us in paradise,
drowned us in wine and concubines,
palaces, gold, and strong scents.
The strawberries from all the way over there,
their fragrance alone sates me.

I'm not saying you lie.
I'm sated and heavy with death.
The children, too,
their dreams are answered
as they run away from school
followed on every street by police patrols,
those children are also full.

I'm full of death and you are as well.
So let's take a rest,
we've fructified the earth.

And after each war,
girls fall in love
with the party's official spokesman,
and we lose the war,
then princes come

to stroke the faces of the ill, kiss their foreheads,
and after the interview
disinfect their hands and go home.

The victors grow victorious,
saturate our heads with speeches and songs.
After the carnival
a boy, in whose face the winners shout
slogans of triumph,
remains alone—
looking for his left hand
in the oration of longing.

—I'm not saying they're telling lies.
But this war's ended,
and someone should gather body parts off trees,
someone should stop clapping,
someone should sweep the dusty streets.

I Don't Believe in Greats

I'm aware some people suffer enough torment to become a lighthouse
then live on to old age
incapable of seeing what lights their way.

I don't believe in survival.
I live in other people's stories
like a rock suspended in space:
it doesn't drop and can't.

And blame, I don't believe in it.
When incidents baffle me
and enemies blur into friends
I keep on filing my nails.
I've never blamed my nails
for nails that tear the flesh on my back.

Each time an opportunity arises for me to not believe in one thing
or another I smile from ear to ear
to let all this freedom in.

Wedding Anniversary

You're not a present.
Love dies. Talk about
contentment is funny,
doesn't ignite the gas stove,
and I don't want an oven for a gift,
no dinner either.
I want to enjoy brushing my teeth
for a whole half hour,
to massage my hands and eyes
with creams and baby oil,
and to watch you stand over there
behind the heavy pressure cooker
for a bit longer.
And since you're not a present,
and it's not my birthday,
I hope you'll feel fulfilled
with some love poems
packed with ludicrous poise
on this pure and holy eve,
because I want to sleep.

Wishes

She wished he'd been the first
she had loved and the last she would love.
The kind of wishes that repeat in love
stories and in stories of death:
"I wish today was the last day of this world
and that you were my final love."
Mere wishes to bombard time with.
Truly infidel wishes—
like wanting to be someone else
with kinder parents
who buy more presents for her
in a house with central heating
and windows overlooking the sea—
blind wishes that don't quit.

She wished it was love
like any love
patting her eyelids in the evening
as she waited on the balcony,
gathering her feelings with invocation,
fragrance, food, and kisses.
A love worth a thousand loves,
a love with two hands.

Trash

All I wanted today
was to sit on the doorstep
and think of you,
but the smell of trash
proposed big
existential questions:
Why did I love you
in February and not in March,
when our wild rosebush, neglected
by the gate, blooms?
Why not when the neighbors' jasmine fills
the street with dreams?
Why not in a different season,
when the entire village,
women, men, children, and dogs,
harvest olives
with their hands and teeth,
and my name on their lips
would urge me to shake
the thickest trunk
with my gnarly incisors
and rapid stirs?
Today, all I wanted
was to sit on the step
and think of you, but now,
whatever you do next March,
and whichever roses and gardens bloom,
the smell of trash will always be with us.

Energy

And because they don't dissipate
or perish,
those things that don't arrive
are placed in the back corners
of memory chambers—
the longing that cold letters digest,
the elegance that house mirrors gobble,
the shoes we kick barefoot,
the wasted sighs
after a pathetic episode
of a romance series on TV—
those things that don't arrive
and are forgotten.
But when their time comes,
as time comes for everything,
we ask with remarkable silliness,
where does all this forgetting come from,
all this crinkling apathy,
the messages that aren't answered,
the turned-off phones,
yellow smiles,
and severed meetings?
From over there, that's where.
From the things that don't dissipate
or perish,
the things that should have arrived
but didn't.

III.

(from *That Smile, That Heart,* 2012)

Mahmoud

Mahmoud could have been our son.
I'd have objected to the name
and, for family reasons, you'd have insisted on it.
We could have bought him a crib with a blue quilt
and hung spinning musical animals
to coax him to sleep,
could have stayed up all night for his first tooth,
experimenting with various formulas
because my breasts couldn't produce enough milk
for his voracious appetite.
And with a new Nikon camera,
we could have captured his first step.
And his verbal skills would have wiped the floor
with your niece's skills, of course.
We could have disagreed over his elementary school:
nothing wrong with public education, you'd have said,
and I'd have demanded a private one.
You'd have turned your face toward me
as you counted our few remaining dollars
to my wailing about balancing the budget.
We would have been happy,
his first school bag in one hand,
his other hand waving to the neighbor's girl
before waving to us.
His teacher would've complained
as teachers are wont to do,
and we'd have called her names for her blindness
to the genius of our only son. Yes,

we would have bought him a battery-operated car,
built him a paper plane that doesn't fly,
maintained his teeth white,
flipped his collar for coolness,
and he'd have loved me more than you
because of issues beyond my grasp:
your jealousy would've grown mysterious.
And when his voice changed he'd hate us both
and love the neighbor's girl more.
Rumination would have haunted us
for hours at night. Our whispers
advising us to be patient, let go, observe
from a distance. Then you'd have lost your wits
over his first cigarette, the hidden pack
in the laundry room, but his tremulous voice
would prevent you from slapping him
with an open palm. You'd have forgiven him,
you're kind like that. He'd only smoked in secret.
But the first rock he'd have thrown
at soldiers at the checkpoint,
to raise his heroic stock in Manal's eyes,
would have declared war in our house:
biting followed by flying slippers.
Nightly debates wouldn't have helped us
to core solutions. I'd have to carry him
between my teeth, fly him
from one neighborhood to another to shield him.
But he'd run away.
That would be who he'd always been.
A misguided kid who saps the heart and soul,

that's who he was. Still you
were martyred eight years
before he was born, and he was martyred
eight years after you were gone.

Children

A child's hand sticks out of the rubble
and sends me counting
my three children's limbs,
their digits, examining their teeth
and eyebrows.

The silenced voices in Yarmouk
turn the volume up on my radio, TV,
and drown the songs on my laptop.
I pinch my kids in their love handles:
let there be crying,
let there be noise.

And the hungry hearts
at Qalandia Checkpoint open my mouth:
I crave salt for my emotional eating
to feed weeping
eyes everywhere.

Elegy for the Desire of Mothers

As I make my bed and my two kids' beds,
I'll remember. As I wipe one's vomit off the floor,
open a window to the dust on the road,
trim rose thorns in a pot that doesn't bud,
and as I read a recipe for authentic *mansaf,*
mend a white gown that little fingers
have ripped holes through,
I'll remember. As I balance winter's budget,
sniff a quilt for ammonia,
flip through the six children's channels
looking for *Tom and Jerry* per request,
and as I search in my supermarket of a purse
for a stray pad, I'll remember.
As I bathe a body the size of my palm,
remove green boogers from tender nostrils,
untangle hair that chocolate, lollipop,
and apricot jam have invaded,
and as I read stories about vibrant ants, lazy lions,
and migrant seals, degum my heart
and the sole of my shoe,
search for the best method
to remove oil stains from fabric,
clip twenty nails after a long quest for clippers,
I'll remember. When a child touches me
innocently in places that no longer work,
when the faucet sprays me, and Turkish soap
operas declare me their number one fan.
When two hands pinch me under the table
in a restaurant. And when I mine

my friends' stories for living desires,
I'll remember to mention them all,
mothers with jaundiced eyes
spilling before me whole,
their dazzling thighs
that defile the house, their fleeting anger
in certain times of the month,
their excessive anxiety over the phone bill,
their belly cramps of endless bloating,
and their interpretation of dreams
for little ridiculous devils,
their coffee cups for fortune-telling,
their song of a blue skirt and a broad knee,
lips that ooze from self-biting,
large bras to safekeep coins and bills,
forgotten aprons over plump guts,
and the nonstop anecdotes
about the licentious girls next door,
mothers
with cut braids
and clay henna on both sides of a face,
and dead desires.

Almost Dead, Almost Alive

Everyone's crossing the streets with their caskets.
They see what I see only by chance,
as when our eyes meet in mirrors or funerals.

Naked I carry my casket on my shoulder,
wear it to soirees and special events,
take it off when I write a poem
about love, war, and heartless images.

Then we meet, Death and I,
on Transmission Street. Audacious
and unexpected, he resembles me. A little black
under the eyes, red near the heart,
and doesn't breathe through his nose.

Who am I when you, Death, are?
Who's your victim and who's my killer?
But death has no sky outside what I speak
and no opinion besides fate or accident.
"That's how distances grow
and shrink between two lives."

If we live, we live lightly
and if we die, we die shyly.
Our road's our shadow, and I'm my road,
the walking on the road, the fleeting flesh,
I'm what I say and claim

and might not be
more than a breath
that passes from you to you,
a carrier of your resident and visiting viruses.

Or maybe I'm a noun sentence
without a subject, only a predicate
marked by inflection. Or maybe I'm not
a dead person who resembles the living,
or a living person who resembles the dead.

I live for a little while longer—
with cosmic concerns,
a modernist sermon, a political affiliation,
a chapeau, beret, eyeliner
and some Nina Ricci perfume.
Necessities to believe
I'm almost dead, almost alive.

Psychology News

Tonight
these things don't wound me:
your player heart, the young women around you,
or that woman who fashions your long day.
It's my belly that weighs me down,
bloated with falafel and banal expressions.

*

Sure, I'm pissed off at a woman who toyed with my blood
and stole your death.

*

She's me. Each time I try to get past myself
I return to zero.
Neither foundation nor green smiles helped me
to resemble other women.
I am an apricot
that did not reach your mouth.

*

I loved the sea at the edge of a map.
It seduced me in geography textbooks.
This is my country, that is my sea,
and here is my elegant lie.

Daydream

I'll write about a joy that invades Jenin from six directions,
about children running while holding balloons in Am'ari Camp,
about a fullness that quiets breastfeeding babies all night in Askar,
about a little sea we can stroll up and down in Tulkarem,
about eyes that stare in people's faces in Balata,
about a woman dancing
for people in line at the checkpoint in Qalandia,
about stitches in the sides of laughing men in Azzoun,
about you and me
stuffing our pockets with seashells and madness
and building a city.

That Smile, That Heart

Little smiles that milk teeth shape,
little smiles that depart
to no return,
smiles that make their rounds in the house,
visit the nice neighbor's shop,
stay on the sidewalk to get to school,
smiles that don't drink milk
and are unharmed by sweets.
But when they depart,
not from caries
and not broken in a pickup
soccer game or from a dentist screwup—
when they leave this world
without growing up into roaring laughter
or kindness to the needy
in the book of good deeds—
when little smiles don't grow
a dream on a lover's pillow
yet depart
with eyes green with hope—
that's when the universe goes quiet
and whimpers.

Empty Repetitive State

1.

The stories I repeat I know by heart.
My lungs are trucks that leak a dying breath.
My armpits exude odorous moisture.
My only sweat is what news has placed
on my cheeks.
My lips are hungry,
they eat my fake smiles at a slow pace.
This isn't happiness
or sadness, exactly
as in the movie with Meg Ryan
that I watched ten times,
perfected its dialogue and next moves,
a romantic film on repeat
to seize on my believability
in a location no audience can doubt,
a site that has no time,
no alarm clock I can shatter.
An empty repetitive state
is me.

2.

I know by heart the stories I repeat.
There's one about my father
guided through the streets by strangers
who wished him dead the day before
when rain caused no head to bleed.

The strangers stretch him where
he brought the *kenafeh* tray,
its syrup and rose water last Eid.
His head was where I sit
staring at the ceiling.
He was mumbling, "Finish your plate."
And as others around him wailed,
he screamed, "Which is it,
a flogging or a feeding?"
I see myself holding back my contempt
for the hundredth time, won't say,
"Gather what you forgot
in my head and leave."
I almost want to say it,
but no voice comes out of me
and no voice returns.
Of all things that depart
the first image lingers.
Of all things that depart
the last image hangs around.
Of all things that arrive,
why doesn't warmth come?

3.

I repeat the stories I know by heart.
Love hangs me in the closet
with a thread of tobacco and perfume.
A photo in some frame
looks like what one day
didn't look like anything:

our love,
a foundation bottle
to break a face
several times over,
a mirror to reveal only the concealed:
my face is a bed of desire,
my laptop hot on my thighs,
my imagination a pair of shoes
the color of trees
while the taste of streets
goes missing, comes back as a towel
wet with longing
after the last shower:
the wetness
doesn't evaporate,
the towel isn't worn out,
my room
is your room,
a bed and a closet,
and whatever else
that doesn't go dry.

I Didn't Love and Wasn't Loved

The distances between you and my needs
wasted me. You didn't open your longing's door
wide enough for the yellow creatures in my blood
to enter, and you didn't force your way in.

My need doesn't pummel my soul.
I'm not looking to die in the rhyme
of bare necessities or some Chopin.

My leaves haven't fallen.
Passersby don't feel for me.
And I didn't turn into an almond blossom to fulfill
your wish for a long embrace.

Over there I stand.
My fingers are conjunction words,
my heart, a poem.
I restore calm to my tiptoes with maroon velvet socks
to imagine warmth
when the only possible warmth
is you on fire
overwhelmed with defeat.

Cold, your coldness, consumes me.
I didn't love and wasn't loved.

I

A dust mote
stuck in an abandoned windowsill.
A crumpled piece of paper in the hands
of children waiting for a bin.
A bird's feather that a feral cat clawed out.
A Macintosh container
empty of chocolate and filled
with spools and needles.
A school uniform after school is out for summer.
A cockroach flipped on its back
pending a broom.

In Love

In love, one loses something.
The other, who loses everything,
deserves the title of lover.

In love, truth is a beautiful illusion.
One will turn this illusion into definite matter.
That one doesn't deserve the title of lover.

In love, despite all the losses, we triumph
over specific things: time, for example,
or boredom, going to bed early, the impossible,
or some nihilism.

In love, one will ask vast existential questions
that no one will have answers to,
while the other watches clouds pass.

IV.

(from *What She Spoke of Him*, 2006)

A Contemporary Novel

heeds no council, offers no raw
solutions, is part and parcel of actions
that were not taken.

Finding out who the killer is
is not the point of the murder
in the opening scene.

For the third time my hands
alter the female protagonist
before the novel even begins.

In her palms his mysterious chiseled form is inspired.

The oracle saw him twice,
cautioned her against caution: "Be him,"
she told her when she noticed fear
in the lumen of narrative asking questions about him.

The female protagonist visits him in the mornings,
taps shyly on the window, sweeps the street with a glance.
(Did anyone see her?)

The plants on the windowsill lean in and bloom for him
then share with her
the waiting and anticipation.

He's the protagonist who doesn't play
his role well: he opens the door,
grumbles about a dream interrupted.

Something has prepared him for absence
but he prolongs her presence with a Raï song:
"I love you, woman."

"He loves me," she smiles to herself.
"She's sweet," he smiles to himself.

My hand takes off the woman's face
and hangs it by the door: "Be good
while I'm gone. Don't make a fuss
over a fleeting present. And if need be
put on a clown's face and don't work yourself up."

The female protagonist doesn't cry
as she shuts the door behind her.
She addresses her grievance to the narrators:
"There's no time on which
my body leans that does not fall.
I don't have what pleases critics.
What remains is chatter."

About Him

On him light gives off no shadow.
Alone, he repeats his sentences
to confirm his existence.
We watched him until he was out of sight
around the corner
in the wholesale farmer's market.
Cats fled him then returned to him,
licked his feet and face.
We didn't mind. It wasn't easy
what he said—or that was
his friends' excuse for their silence
as they sat together sipping
ginger tea in the evening.

*

In my hands I prepared everything he needed to be.
I was drowning up to my fingertips
in intention
and didn't survive.

*

Behind the curtain I was covered, he was not.
It was the curse of the vine,
said the fortune-teller. Behind the curtain
we felt fortunate yet concerned
with the scandal of his exposure.
Why him? The question didn't matter,

we didn't care for an answer
that might elevate him and distance us.
We tossed our shameful panting his way.
Like an excited crowd before a stoning.

*

By the wall of books I opened the first page of desire.
He was a wild lover with no time
to read the footnotes
though I'd wanted a longer scene
in which he's not the only protagonist.
I took off my pantyhose and danced.
I was beautiful, and he was a beast
who didn't understand time's tricks.

*

Every myth expelled him.
He was a demigod, didn't comply
with the contemporary requirement
for metamorphosis.
He was the mysterious project
of the ceiling bearer
and was the only one who recalled
where the compass was kept.

The Upcoming Dervish Dance

Folds wrap him as if a snake,
expose years of local poison
in the hour of harvest.
He crouches in a text from the language of exile
like a god
plays a flute, scarfs
himself with mysterious quotes of some poets.
He disappears to return
from the demon's belly
as a lantern—to fulfill
with his split flail lower lip
his ten or hundred wishes.

Madness advocates for truth.
Under the scorching sun
he disappears to return
as a firstborn from a woman's lap.
He craves the insane silence before and after love,
the absurd magic in the swallow of a kiss.

Folds besiege him, bear his sixty losses.
At dawn they came to his door,
led him with his rattling snake to a forest
whose bark nurtures no leaves.
No firmament descended to his grass,
no dew for his blood in the mud.

Speech nagged his lips, ran with rain raging
in the forest where insects and rodents,

attracted by the lie
of human misery and happiness,
came to his eyes.

In his room, a universe.
He crouches, hugs
his sculpted leg, dwells in himself.
They came before dawn
bearing a time that tasted drowsy and drunk.
He apologized
to the color of wine
and the warmth of sleep among other things
he didn't reveal, didn't know
what to say
before he covered his dreams
with burlap.

Maybe summer came suddenly.
He predicted the hues
that will flow in his hair.
Gray wears the upcoming dervish dance.

What She Left in You

At the table I take off my hand, learn to love outside time.
The bottle doesn't contain my limbs (or mind and soul).
I struggle outside me
inside you. The bottle
with sagging chest doesn't spill me in a prefilled planner.
How do I access my waiting
when all the seats are taken.

*

Now I am the last of light and know no one beside you.
Make some room for warmth near your bed
so that your steps on my face wake me in the morning.
The space between my lips
is about to give birth
to a barren mother.

*

Sex: I knew it twice.
Once in ecstasy's horror
and another through your sweat.
Each instance, I cried.
Each instance, the hegemonic place
slapped my heart.
The difference is a stranger to me.

*

Whenever happiness surrounds your halo
you close your eyes and grow sad.
Did you know that dialogue is led by two:
you and what she left in you?
Open your eyes.
There are things I want to say still.

The Looming Wide Path

No face resembles the photos my hands hid
of this looming conceit.

I don't quite catch my hair
or the rustle in my voice.
I'm the saline earth that walks on the curb,
surveys the city's crowds
in a tourist summer packed with travel.

My mother fixes her hair in the mirror, goes out
for a jog. No holy shadows over her motherhood

no more, while on the sidewalk
I swing near and far. I resemble her
when the fever of wrinkles and neck folds
afflicts me, and when this looming wide path
is humorless and tells no tales.

Did you put on sunscreen? she asks from her distance.
I check my forehead, recall that I left
my face on the coat hanger before I left the house.

I tell her this as she continues her jog and grows
smaller, smaller.

Acknowledgments

AGNI: "Fear"

Asymptote Journal: "My House," "A Road for Loss," "What If," "Like a Domestic Animal," "Similarities"

Baffler: "A Contemporary Novel"

Cordite Poetry Review: "Penniless," "Since They Told Me My Love Won't Be Coming Back from the War," "I Don't Believe in Greats"

Los Angeles Review of Books: "We," "I Don't Ask Anymore," "Massacres," "You Can't"

New York Review of Books: "I Burn Time"

Waxwing: "The Kids Are Screaming Now," "Revolution," "Elegy for the Desire of Mothers"

Maya Abu Al-Hayyat

Maya Abu Al-Hayyat is the director of the Palestine Writing Workshop, an institution that seeks to encourage reading in Palestinian communities through creative writing projects and storytelling with children and teachers. She has published four collections of poems, four novels, and numerous children's stories, including *The Blue Pool of Questions*. She contributed to and wrote a foreword for *A Bird Is Not a Stone: An Anthology of Contemporary Palestinian Poetry*, and she is also an editor of *The Book of Ramallah*. Her work has appeared in the *Los Angeles Review of Books*, *Cordite Poetry Review*, *The Guardian*, and Literary Hub. Abu Al-Hayyat lives in Jerusalem and works in Ramallah.

Cybele Knowles

Fady Joudah has published five collections of poems: *The Earth in the Attic*; *Alight*; *Textu*, a book-long sequence of short poems whose meter is based on cellphone character count; *Footnotes in the Order of Disappearance*; and, most recently, *Tethered to Stars*. He has translated several collections of poetry from the Arabic and is the co-editor and co-founder of the Etel Adnan Poetry Prize. He was a winner of the Yale Series of Younger Poets competition in 2007 and has received a PEN award, a Banipal/Times Literary Supplement prize from the UK, the Griffin Poetry Prize, and a Guggenheim Fellowship. He is an Editor-at-Large for Milkweed Editions. He lives in Houston, with his wife and kids, where he practices internal medicine.

milkweed
editions

Founded as a nonprofit organization in 1980, Milkweed
Editions is an independent publisher. Our mission is to
identify, nurture and publish transformative literature,
and build an engaged community around it.

Milkweed Editions is based in Bdé Óta Othúŋwe
(Minneapolis) within Mní Sota Makhóčhe, the traditional
homeland of the Dakhóta people. Residing here since time
immemorial, Dakhóta people still call Mní Sota Makhóčhe
home, with four federally recognized Dakhóta nations and
many more Dakhóta people residing in what is now the state
of Minnesota. Due to continued legacies of colonization,
genocide, and forced removal, generations of Dakhóta people
remain disenfranchised from their traditional homeland.
Presently, Mní Sota Makhóčhe has become a refuge and
home for many Indigenous nations and peoples, including
seven federally recognized Ojibwe nations. We humbly
encourage our readers to reflect upon the historical legacies
held in the lands they occupy.

milkweed.org

Interior design by Tijqua Daiker
Typeset in Jenson

Adobe Jenson was designed by Robert Slimbach for Adobe
and released in 1996. Slimbach based Jenson's roman styles
on a text face cut by fifteenth-century type designer Nicolas
Jenson, and its italics are based on type created by Ludovico
Vicentino degli Arrighi, a late fifteenth-century
papal scribe and type designer.

Milkweed Editions, an independent nonprofit publisher, gratefully acknowledges sustaining support from our Board of Directors; the Alan B. Slifka Foundation and its president, Riva Ariella Ritvo-Slifka; the Amazon Literary Partnership; the Ballard Spahr Foundation; *Copper Nickel*; the McKnight Foundation; the National Endowment for the Arts; the National Poetry Series; the Target Foundation; and other generous contributions from foundations, corporations, and individuals. Also, this activity is made possible by the voters of Minnesota through a Minnesota State Arts Board Operating Support grant, thanks to a legislative appropriation from the arts and cultural heritage fund. For a full listing of Milkweed Editions supporters, please visit milkweed.org.